ENTHRONED

A 14-DAY GUIDE TO INTERIOR REVOLUTION AND A LIFE OF PRAYER

i

Imprimatur: Printed With Ecclesiastical Permission. Most Reverend Earl Boyea.
May 16, 2017.

Printed in the United States of America

ISBN: 978-0-692-87712-8

Thank you to Kelly Hanshaw for editorial work
and Abby Feldpausch for layout and design.
To both of you: Your work and sacrifice in helping me
prepare this resource have been an inspiration.

Thank you to my wife and children.
You have revealed God to me in a way few can.

INTRODUCTION

We are in desperate need of revolution in the world today. Everywhere we turn we encounter some form of war, whether it is with weapons, or with words, or with actions. Humanity is turned against itself and in on itself. There are wars being waged on women, men, babies, children, families, race, religion, and sexuality and it just seems to be escalating the more our culture buys into the self-serving ideas that relativism,[1] and a culture without a single point of origin, produce. It all leads to chaos – and we are seeing that now.

This culture is toxic and needs to be changed. But do you see yourself in your current state a fit instrument to change it? The truth is that a lot of us have the same battles we see in the culture around us happening within us. We are just as volatile inside as the culture is outside. So how are we going to change the culture if we ourselves need so much changing? The answer is portrayed in the life of Jesus himself – *Prayer.*

Prayer is one thing that with time, and a heart and mind resolved to the pursuit of it, can actually change us to be fit instruments of a cultural revolution; a revolution that can and will sweep the world just as the early Christians did to the Roman culture of the time.

Think about it, Christianity claims what seeks to destroy it. The Romans were the ones who hung Jesus on the cross, and at that moment I suppose they thought that they had won and crushed this whole *"Jesus movement"*. However, God has a way of taking those who give themselves entirely over to Him, and raising them up to turn a culture on its head. I suppose the Romans also thought they won when they crucified Peter upside down in what is now referred to as Saint Peter's square. That day it appeared they won, but fast forward only a couple hundred years and the capital of Rome starts becoming the capital of

---

[1] Relativism: The belief that different things are true, right, etc., for different people or at different times (*Merriam-Webster*)

Christianity and a basilica is raised that bears the name of Peter, and still stands to this day. It is from this basilica that the Pope and bishops guide the Catholic Church and the faithful to Christ.

Where sin abounds grace abounds all the more (Romans 5:20). Take this time of grace and start using it to redefine yourself. Start to see yourself as just as capable of being a great saint as the early Christians were. Do not limit what God can do with you.

God is not dead. He is very much alive and He is looking for people who are willing to give their hearts and minds over to Him daily in prayer, to be transformed by Him, and in turn be sent out to transform the world. He wants to start a revolution in you so that you can then take that revolution out to the world, and be a fit instrument in His hands, ready to do what are truly His works.

Who knows what the world will look like in two thousand years? Today could be the start of its transformation in you. Submit yourself to interior revolution – submit yourself to prayer.

GOAL

The goal of this resource is to provide practical steps to a prayer life through everyday considerations and practice of prayer oriented to the exploration of the interior life. It is setup to start out more rigid, with clear steps and thoughts, but as it goes on it becomes a lot more about your own words with God, and His own words back to you. By the end of this it is my hope that, after gaining knowledge and practice of prayer, you will feel comfortable to continue on your journey and life of intimacy with God.

It may help to think about it this way: if you are really interested in someone and want to get to know them better, often times mutual friends can help bring the both of you together. Maybe you go out on a couple of group dates in order to ease into conversation, and to find common ground through common friends. Then, when it is just the two of you, the conversation is not so awkward. You kind of already have some ideas of where to go with things, and there is a comfort level there that would not have been if it weren't for the mutual friends that brought the both of you together.

This resource is to be used in much the same way. Let it just serve as an intermediary for your relationship with God for a bit (although the ideas covered, much like your mutual friends, will not go away). Hopefully it helps alleviate some of the awkwardness, and helps bring you to a better understanding of each other quicker. Follow the steps and then, just as if you were out on a group date, let your gaze start going more and more on the one who you intend to be with, and start leaving behind the rigidity of the prescribed words, and start forming your own.

This is about your relationship with Him. The purpose of this is to facilitate the growth of that relationship.

This book is setup with considerations followed by a time of prayer. This is so because any life of prayer is accompanied by study (consideration) and most often times the study is what enriches the time of prayer and keeps your heart and mind moving toward a more intimate time in prayer. Just like with any relationship, the more we come to know the other person, the more intimate and meaningful our time spent with them can be. Never stop your study; it will do so much to enrich your mind in prayer.

A simple exploration of the interior life can help us take the first steps to the realization of God as our Father. Not just intellectually understanding it – but interiorly knowing it. This realization then informs our heart and mind in the ways we approach God throughout the day and most especially in prayer. The more we pray the more our understanding of God's fatherly role deepens and we can respond by allowing Him to teach us deeply in His ways – to rear us as His children. This is the journey of the soul.

TABLE OF CONTENTS

Set aside a minimum of 15 minutes for each day's readings and prayer.

PREPARATION:

Note: If you use this time and do what is recommended you will see it pay dividends during the times of prayer. The prep will allow your mind to focus more during the time of prayer because many concerns that would have arisen will already be taken care of. Anything we do in life that is worth doing we make preparations for; prayer is no different.

EXPLORING THE INTERIOR LIFE:

ADDITIONAL READING:

Note: All bible citations are taken from the New American Bible.

DAY 1: PLACE AND TIME | PREPARATION

FIND AND PREPARE A PLACE IN YOUR HOME

The first thing you need to do to get started is to prepare a place in your home where you can consistently meet God in prayer. Make sure this place allows for quiet time where you can be alone. When considering your place of prayer you should consider some of these things:

- Will this place lend itself to few interruptions?
- Am I easily distracted in this place?
- Is it too bright, bringing my attention to other things in the room?
- Can I be comfortable there?
- Does it lend itself well to sitting and writing?

The dining room table is a fitting spot for me to pray early in the morning because no one else is up in my family, and the table and chairs allow me to be comfortable while reading and writing. See an image of the space below. This is just to show you how simple your area can be.

FIGURE OUT A TIME THAT WORKS BEST

Time-of-day is a big consideration here as well. The time you set aside every day to do this will largely influence the number of distractions you could come against. I have found the only way I can guarantee consistency in being able to secure an undistracted place, is early morning before anyone else in my family is up. Depending on your work/family schedule this may not be possible. I would then recommend that you figure something out at night, a lunch break, or another time where you can be uninterrupted.

It is good for your household if your prayer life does not become a burden on the other members of your family. For instance, if I plan on praying every day right when I get home from work it might irk my wife a bit that I come home and immediately request quiet time away, especially when there are kids involved. Think about how this will affect the dynamic of your home life. Try to be as little of a burden on others with this as you can, so there is not discouragement from anyone outside of yourself. Trust me, we have enough of a challenge overcoming ourselves.

I know some may be thinking, *"This sounds like quite a commitment. I already don't have enough time in my day. How am I supposed to fit prayer in as well?"* Let me tell you, pretty much everyone I know struggles with this same dilemma. Especially when it comes to trying to find time amid a busy family life. The thing we really have to consider is that our lives are not made to serve our own needs. Our lives are made for relationship with God and to serve His Kingdom. If we look at our lives in this light, then getting up and blindly walking into our day without first spending time with Him and seeing what He wants of us, seems just about the farthest thing from what we should do. It is not prayer that needs to be worked into our lives, but rather our lives need to be worked around prayer.

I am reminded of a story Mother Teresa told about her Missionaries of Charity routine. She said that one day she was approached by some of her fellow Missionaries of Charity and they asked her if they could get an hour of adoration added to their daily routine. Mother was over-whelmed at first, and didn't know how to fit such a request into their already busy schedule that saw them rise early and retire late. After much prayer, she decided it was a good thing to give the sisters that extra time to be with Jesus in adoration and she entrusted their work to the Lord even more so they could keep up. She found that when they instituted that hour of adoration and prayer for the sisters their days seemed to be more productive. They were able to get all of their labors accomplished in the day just as they were able to before the hour was added.

This is truly remarkable. You would think that if you took an hour away from your work day you would see a decline in output, and that it would be the same way with adding consistent prayer time to your life. The difference is that we were not made for busyness but we were made for union with God. As Pope Benedict XVI said in his *Jesus of Nazareth* Series, "Man is a relational being. And if his first, fundamental relationship is disturbed – his relationship with God – then nothing else can be truly in order." (44)

So God, being who He is, can make your time more productive when you give your first fruits of it to Him. He is a God of multiplication and simplification. He is not afraid to multiply your output for those things that need to get done, and to simplify your life so that those things that you once thought mattered – that you couldn't give up – are of no avail. You just find yourself, in the light of prayer, not caring about them.

Another common thing I hear, and I am guilty of this from time to time is; "I am already tired enough. If I wake up early to start my day with prayer I will be all the more tired." I don't know how to explain this, but this is not true. The days when I sleep past my alarm and miss prayer are the days when I am the most tired and irritable. However, on the days I make that time in the morning to spend with God, and seek what He wants from me, I feel happier and often more awake. It is a mystery, but I think it goes back to what Pope Benedict said, that once our relationship with

God is in proper order, everything in our lives start to fall more gracefully into place. Peace starts to envelope us, even amid the storm.

One last thought: God knows how important your time is even more than you do. He is the only one aware of the amount of it that you have left. He respects your time and does great things with it once you just start giving Him some of it.

ITEMS TO FOCUS ON THROUGHOUT THE DAY

• Prepare a place in your home where you can pray

• Think of a good time that will work for you
(first thing in the morning is preferred)

• Foster belief in God's providence for your time

DAY 2: DISTRACTIONS | PREPARATION

DISTRACTIONS OUTSIDE OF PRAYER TIME

Catechism of the Catholic Church (CCC) paragraph 2725: "Prayer is a battle. Against whom? Against ourselves and against the wiles of the tempter who does all he can to turn man away from prayer, away from union with God. "

There are so many distractions that grip our hearts and our minds outside of prayer and take us away from that time of intimacy with God. As the Catechism states above, we have two main enemies in this battle: ourselves and the tempter (the devil).

One battle we often fight within ourselves is the battle for our comfort. We like to be comfortable, and we like to justify a lack of prayer in our lives in favor of that comfort. A life of prayer requires discipline – always. Discipline also encompasses patience and a realistic view of our situation, so we are not called to become "Navy Seals of prayer" overnight; rather, it is a journey that sees a lot of ups and downs. The most important thing is that tomorrow sees us giving prayer an effort and recommitting ourselves to a relationship with our Lord.

Hopefully you already have your prayer spot selected in your home, and have started acquiring the items you need that will make it a comfortable place where you can focus on God. This is huge. If we know we can get right to that place and have very little to do to prepare it then we are countering our desire for comfort. We actually work within that desire because that place is now comfortable.

We have an amazing ability to justify a move toward comfort, especially early in the morning. For most this is the best opportunity to secure quiet time in their busy homes. However, a tired mind likes to make a tired hand hit the snooze button, and before you know it, the time you had set aside for prayer got a lot shorter, and before too long you are sleeping right through it. It is really important to build resolve to make that time of prayer work. A good exercise is to think about it before you go to bed and build up a desire to get up that next morning. This little exercise does a lot to get your mind on the right track when your alarm goes off. Do as much as you can to overcome your desire for comfort when it opposes your prayer and ask God for an abundance of graces to combat it.

The distractions the enemy brings up seem to be geared more toward a downturn in our emotional state regarding prayer, sometimes to the point of feeling resentment toward it. Your mind can feel clouded and dark, and he can use this to curb your resolve to pray just enough to then get out of the way and let your own desire for comfort take over. It is very important to pray against this. Call on your guardian angel, Mary, and all the saints to safeguard your prayer life from the wiles of the devil. A couple of examples of prayers you could use would be:

Lord, I am being tempted away from you. I reject this. Bring me back to You.

Mother Mary, my Guardian Angel, St Michael and all saints and angels, I ask that you guard me from the temptations and snares of the devil and that you free me to have a relationship with our Lord as you have. That I may do His will and accomplish my life's task. In Jesus' name.

The bottom line is that your prayer life will come under attack – because the devil knows that prayer is the one thing that will guide you in the ways that you are supposed to walk. It will destroy his plans for your life, because you will start to know the Heart of God, and the devil and his temptations to sin will become so much less attractive. Fight for your time of prayer. Without it you will not be able to become who you were made to be.

One final note on the place of prayer, if you have kids or a busy home do not be afraid of the occasional interruption from a waking kid or spouse. While you don't want this happening all of the time, it is not bad to have your kids wake up and see the example of you starting your day out with prayer. If my children get up, I will normally invite them over, and try to read the day's gospel to them, and ask them to say a prayer with me for the day. This can go from feeling like an interruption to being a great way for you to foster a life of prayer for your children and those you care about. They will never learn prayer's proper place unless you show them.

DISTRACTIONS WITHIN PRAYER TIME

Now that you hopefully have a place in mind where you will be praying it is good to think about the distractions that you may encounter in that place – not to get overly worried about them, but to work to eliminate or manage them before they derail your time of prayer. These could be a number of things. Depending on your space, it could be the lighting is too bright and your eyes keep wandering to items that are distracting you or causing your mind to drift. In this situation I have found that a low light source really helps. Candles, oil lamps, or dim lamps really seem to help pull our minds in to be just in the space we are in. It could also be that the space is too noisy or cluttered, which can bring your mind to focus on those things.

Something to consider is getting yourself an item that you are excited about to have in your prayer area. (Crucifix, mug, nice pen, nice journal...) This can help you on those days where your will to pray is not so strong, to make time for it because of excitement about the item. For me that was a new coffee maker; there have been many mornings that the comfort of a cup of coffee has helped me bridge the gap of the desire to get up when it wasn't completely there. God is the source of all of these things and if we orient them to serve our coming to Him then they are being properly used.

You should prepare for prayer the same way you would prepare for a work related activity, or anything of high importance to you. At work you would have some coffee to stay awake so you can get your work done. The same should be done for your time of prayer; if you find yourself consistently falling asleep, then do what is necessary to stay awake. If you find that you are cold and it is distracting you from prayer, then make sure to set a sweatshirt out to be able to put on to alleviate your drifting mind. This may seem rudimentary and silly, but it seems that little things like these often times can turn into reasons why we stop praying, or they can be causes of great distraction. The point is that prayer is the most important thing you can start in your life. All other conviction will flow from this time – so protect it and play to your strengths with it as much as you can.

When you are in prayer and distractions come up don't try to simply ignore them by your own power. You are in the process of communing with the God of the universe so realize that He has the power to deliver you from them. Go to Him with confidence in His ability to overcome them in you. He does not want any distractions during this time either, as He knows that carving time out of your day for prayer is hard at first.

A humble heart's first inclination is to go to God for help, realizing that apart from him we can do nothing

JOURNALING – AN ENEMY OF DISTRACTION

I highly recommend getting a separate prayer journal. There are many reasons why journaling is so helpful during prayer, but one of the main reasons is that it is a great combat to distraction. When prayerfully reading through the day's scripture reading or meditation, the Holy Spirit will often make a phrase or idea stand out to you. It is almost like this phrase becomes bolded in the text or like the words are coming through louder in your heart. These are the words that you want to write down in your journal. Then ask God to inspire your mind and heart to go deeper with these words to better know Him.

What follows is normally a period of writing and reflecting. It is good to write down the thoughts that are coming during this period. This allows our minds to have more focus on the thoughts that are coming. If a fleeting thought comes into mind that would take our mind away from the depth of where God was taking us, as soon as we realize what is happening, we can reference back to what we have written and it can serve to bring our mind back on track and continue on to even greater depths. As long as we have the whereabouts to notice we are distracted, what we have written can draw us back to God and where he seeks to take us in prayer.

Journaling allows us to go deeper with our thoughts even if distraction does not come into play. Writing makes our thoughts and affections more cohesive, and they seem to flow more easily to depths to which they have never traveled before. It can help take what was once an abstract reading, and trace it back to truth, or a certain characteristic of God.

Be sure to Journal during this. You will find that it will bear much fruit in your pursuit of a relationship with God.

ITEMS TO FOCUS ON THROUGHOUT THE DAY

• Think about the distractions that may come up in your home and prayer area and try to work to alleviate them before they become an issue

• Foster belief in God's ability to help you in your busyness and distractions

DAY 3: EXPECTATIONS | PREPARATION

CASTING ASIDE OUR EXPECTATIONS

Throughout all of history, mankind has been expecting things of God. We place our expectations on Him, and then make judgments about His character and the way He acts based on whether or not those expectations are met. Is this fair for us to do? If God really is who He says He is, and He really spoke you into existence and He has loved you and the thought of you for all eternity, do you think that our judgments are correctly rooted? Or do you think that our expectations could be off?

Our expectations help us form judgments, and this is not altogether a bad thing. However, when we are forming judgments against an eternal and infinite being we leave very little space for Him to work in us, and for Him to act in our lives in the way that would best suit us at the given time. In other words, when we, who are finite and limited beings place our expectations on God, who is infinite and unlimited, our expectations actually limit what He can do in us, or at least what we can realize He is doing in us. We tend to obsess over our ideal encounter with Him, and forsake the moment He is giving us. We do not trust that He might actually know what is best for our eternal self to receive in that moment. Maybe if He would give us exactly what we want it would inflate us with pride so that we could not be effective in the future events of our lives.

Expectations are not all bad. For instance, expecting God to do something great is always fitting, but it hinges on what you perceive to be great. If greatness has a minimum of an outer body experience, then you are going to be let down and your expectations are going to blind you to the way God works. If you see the cross as greatness, and the entry of it into your life as a chance to claim greatness, then you will have more accurate and healthy expectations.

When Jesus first entered our world, the expectations of the Jews of the time were at a feverish pitch; they knew the promised Messiah would come soon. Many of them expected a great King that would rule the Kingdom of Israel with military might that has never been matched. He would expand the boundaries of the kingdom to the ends of the Earth. However, what they received was anything but what was expected – a baby like any other in appearance came into the world, born in a manger with the animals. He was not even born in a building occupied by men, but by animals. In a real way the expectations for the messiah at the time made it so there was no room for Him in the world. The lack of physical room in the buildings that people occupied in Bethlehem was an outward visible sign of the lack of room that was being allowed for God in the hearts of those people awaiting Him. Would they be able to accept a helpless infant as their king? Or was that just too far out of the realm of their expectations?

He came nonetheless, and allowed himself to be moved by His creation. The beings that were sustained in life by Him were the very ones that pushed Him out of the town of Bethlehem. Wouldn't we think that God would have come and rolled over anyone who tried to conquer Him? Instead, He made himself reliant on His creation to the point that if Joseph had somehow misinterpreted the dream to leave Bethlehem because King Herod wanted to destroy the baby Jesus, He no doubt would have perished with the other innocent baby boys that were ordered to be killed by Herod (Matthew 2:13).

He did not come to assert himself over his creation; rather, he came to be among them, feeling their pain, crying with them, laughing with them, baring the monotony of daily labor, and above all dying with us. He came and went through just about every inconvenient thing you could ever think about happening in your life. He did this, not to eventually take a throne or palace here on earth in a physical way, He did it so He and the Father in the love of the Holy Spirit could live in those who would be baptized and accept Him forever. He came to be with us and to love us. What more could we expect?

What is more desirable for us than an embrace from someone we care deeply about? This is what Jesus came to bring to the world – an embrace from our creator and an invitation to accept a still more excellent way. He seeks to help us let down our guard and perfect our expectations so we can allow Him to be God and allow ourselves to be His beloved Sons and Daughters.

If we had the choice, most of us would opt that every time we pray God would give us a mystical experience; something that would take us out of our body and be somewhat other worldly. If God acted in this way though, He knows that we would become far more addicted to the sensations of those moments rather than turning more toward Him. We tend to focus on the blessing God gives us so much that the blessing risks becoming a distraction to our relationship with Him. The blessings we receive should serve as a light to illuminate the path to our God, who is so much greater than any consolation we can experience here on earth. Allow yourself to get caught up in Him and be open to the ways He wishes to move, and be assured that His ways are always in your best interest. Allow Him to Father you how He will. He is the best Father any soul could ask for, and *He is yours.*

ITEMS TO FOCUS ON THROUGHOUT THE DAY

• Foster an openness to whatever God wants
to do with you in your prayer time

• Contemplate his infinite life, and ponder this phrase:

"For as the heavens are higher than the earth, so are my ways higher than your ways and my thoughts than your thoughts."
(ISAIAH 55:9)

DAY 4: REFLECT AND RESOLVE | PREPARATION

CLEANSING THE TEMPLE

Reference: Matthew 21:12, Mark 11:15, Luke 19:45, John 2:13

One of the stories in scripture that has always sort of bewildered me in the New Testament is the account of Jesus cleansing the temple. This event happens in all four gospels, and all of them portray it much the same way – Jesus, who is normally calm and generally even keeled, is moved with zeal when he sees many in the temple selling animals for sacrifice and converting currency for the temple tax, so much so that he starts turning over their tables and driving them out. He does this in John's account with a whip! Wait, Jesus? You mean the same Jesus who had said, "let the children come to me," and seemed to have a calm collected answer for just about everything that was brought to Him? This is also the Jesus that healed many and raised a man from the dead? Why is He acting so weird in the temple? This seems really out of character for Him... it seems like He is willing to do just about anything to get these people out of the temple. Read John's account of this below:

John 2:13-17

[13] *Since the Passover of the Jews was near, Jesus went up to Jerusalem.* [14] *He found in the temple area those who sold oxen, sheep, and doves, as well as the money-changers seated there.* [15]*He made a whip out of cords and drove them all out of the temple area, with the sheep and oxen, and spilled the coins of the money-changers and overturned their tables,* [16]*and to those who sold doves he said, "Take these out of here, and stop making my Father's house a marketplace."* [17]*His disciples recalled the words of scripture, "Zeal for your house will consume me."*

The Temple in Jerusalem was the place where God actually dwelt with the Israelites. It was there where they could feel union with God, and where God would make himself known physically in the form of the Shekinah (or glory cloud). It was also there where they could make their prayers known, and offer sacrifice for their sins against God. With these things in mind it makes sense that Jesus, as the Son of God, would have love for the place where He and His Father, along with the Spirit, would dwell and that He would want it to be kept tidy; although it doesn't appear that is entirely why Jesus seemingly flew off the handle. I think it goes deeper.

What Saint Paul writes in his first letter to the Corinthians seems to be the key that unlocks the seemingly erratic behavior of Jesus:

1 Corinthians 3:16-17

[16] Do you not know that you are the temple of God, and that the Spirit of God dwells in you? [17] If anyone destroys God's temple, God will destroy that person; for the temple of God, which you are, is holy."

What could he mean when he says we are the "Temple of God?" Paul is referring here to our hearts, which are made for God alone. You see the temple was just a building that was on the Earth for a limited amount of time. God never intended to come to Earth and occupy a fancy building for the rest of His stay; no, the building only existed to show us through this physical dwelling what He intended to be to us from all eternity. Just like He was actually present in the Temple in Jerusalem, so He intended through His son to become ever present in the hearts of all of those who believe.

Think about it: Jesus knew the Temple would be destroyed in about 40 years with the Roman siege of Jerusalem in 70 AD. Do you really think that His first care was getting the temple in order just to be demolished shortly after?

Jesus's zeal and seemingly erratic behavior is actually because He is fighting for us. We are the "temple" that is causing this behavior. He knows that we become easily distracted and that, instead of using the time we have for constructive things that are actually going to feed us, like prayer, we often just occupy ourselves with busyness.

In this time, only second to the cross, Jesus is imaging His Father. This isn't crazy behavior either. We know that if a parent has lost a child, or a child is kidnapped, the parent will stop at very little to get them back. He isn't crazy – He is imaging God the father in a very raw and real way.

Jesus' cleansing of the temple and His passion are deeply linked. The same passion that He had while overturning tables in the temple was the same passion that He had carrying His cross toward Calvary. What parent wouldn't go to death to get their child back? Jesus' passion, in light of the temple cleansing shows us that even if the soldiers weren't there whipping Him, He would have marched toward His death anyway if it meant saving His Father's beloved children.

The amazing part about this is that nothing has changed from then until now. What He did physically and outwardly for us at that time He is still doing spiritually in us. Jesus is still breaking into people's lives to rid them of their idols and strip them of their busyness, and help them re-orient their lives for the better. There is a catch however – He will not impose himself on you. You need to be willing to let Him into your heart, your temple, and let Him overturn some things and make way for the one who will bring your entire being back into order. He is not without power in us when we call on Him and freely allow Him to have His way in us. Believe He can overcome whatever is built up against Him in you. Give Him permission.

ITEM TO FOCUS ON THROUGHOUT THE DAY

• Extend trust to Jesus that He can overcome whatever has overcome you.

DAY 5: MECHANISMS AND FLOW OF PRAYER | PREPARATION

FLOW OF PRAYER (THIS WILL BE APPLIED TO EACH DAY)

As you are working through this resource, you will find considerations which are then followed by scriptures passages, or other inspired works. The considerations are meant to prepare your mind and your heart to start thinking deeper, and to start drawing yourself to your interior place where prayer finds its origin.

It is recommended that you read through the consideration carefully, seeking understanding and allowing it to help you explore within yourself what it is referring to. After this, we will move onto the prayer section where you will be able to practice *Lectio Divina*, which is prayerful reading of the scriptures, seeking understanding from God.

Below is a formula for prayer that has been time tested and proven worthy of practice. You may have heard it referred to as Guigo's Ladder *(ref page 19).*

> **READ IT (READ)** – Read the scripture passage seeking understanding. This orients us to first listen to God and what He is trying to say to us
>
> *Practical Application – read slowly and thoroughly seeking understanding with an openness to the promptings of the Holy Spirit. (Lectio Divina)*
>
> **MEDITATE ON IT (MEDITATION)** – This can be compared to chewing on the scripture passage with your mind, and with the guidance of the Holy Spirit, so as to draw out its flavor and meaning for you in your life. Since the word of God is living, every scripture passage can speak to us and be relevant in our lives today.
>
> *Practical Application – Explore the meaning of the reading as it applies to your day as well as what it might mean in your*

ENTHRONED

life. Be open to the prompting of the Spirit and see where God may be leading you (journaling helps in this step).

TALK TO HIM ABOUT IT (PRAY) – This is where we start communicating with God. It is our response to our listening and seeking understanding (first two steps). We are then drawn in to conversation with God; we ask Him and seek all the more to understand His ways.

Practical Application – This is simply your inspired conversation, after listening and meditating on His word. (Journaling helps in this step)

BE DRAWN TO HIM (CONTEMPLATION) – This is the lifting up of the heart to God, tasting somewhat of the Heavenly sweetness and savors. It is an invitation from God into His Interior life for a time. (If this happens, do not be afraid to put down your pen and go with God to where He is taking you).

Contemplation can look and feel different at various stages of your spiritual life. At times you may have physical feelings associated with it, like sensations of heat, electricity, and tingling. You may even receive images or visions. At other times you may just have a sense of God's presence. Still, at other times it may feel like extremely focused meditation. The line between meditation and contemplation is sometimes hard to discern. Saint Teresa of Avila experienced levitation at times when caught up to God in contemplation. Although what happened to Saint Teresa is not common, it is ultimately up to God to give you what you need in this time, so don't rule anything out as long as it incites peace interiorly.

LIVE IT – (An added step to conclude time of prayer) Prayer is not an end to itself; rather, it is a conversation and meeting with the one who created you. It should pull you out of yourself and challenge you to start living in the light of The One whom you have been with. It is good to make a resolution for the day – something inspired by your prayer that you can practically apply so that your prayer may not be in vain, but that it may flow into your day by your actions. Keep it simple.

It would be good to read through the above several times and really think of what should be done in each of the steps. To know the steps well would be of help to you, as they will be more easily practiced if they are understood beforehand. Think of it like a tool you are seeking to use: If someone hands you a tool that you have never seen before to accomplish a task, the task might get done, but it will be slow and sluggish, as your understanding of the tool and its use is being formed. However, if you get time to study the tool before the task is presented to you, you will be able to carry out the task more efficiently and gracefully since you already know the tool that is useful for accomplishing it. You can then put all of your concentration on the task at hand, and use the tool more as a utility to the task.

It may help to write these steps down on a loose sheet of paper so you can quickly reference them as you go through the exercises.

Know that God can take you through whatever steps He would like. If it seems you are being taken through these in a different order or skipping some of them, go where God is taking you. This is only a means to the end of encountering God; only a tool to help you get there. If you are already there, then set the tool aside.

GUIGO'S LADDER

These steps can flow in and out of each other.
Do not be afraid to repeat steps.

HEAVENLY THINGS ⟶

CONTEMPLATION

PRAYER

MEDITATION

READING

EARTHLY THINGS ⟶

LIVE IT sends us out to the world with something to act on from our prayer

(ref Ladder page 61).

19

THE INTERIOR LIFE

By starting your day with prayer, that which you thought was reality starts to corrode under the weight of truth. You will find it increasingly easier, because of this newfound truth, to march into the day waving the flag for Jesus Christ in all Love.

PRAYER BEFORE STARTING

Mother Mary and (My favorite Saint), please pray for me to God that, throughout this prayer retreat, the Lord may open my mind and my heart to experience Him in new ways, and that my relationship with Him becomes more real than my relationship with even my closest friend, and that He occupies the throne of my heart.

I entrust my growth to you.

DAY 6: THE THRONE OF OUR HEARTS | THE INTERIOR LIFE

"Come Holy Spirit, inspire my heart and my mind. Bring me to the Heart of God."

CONSIDERATION

Prayer, simply stated, is your heart uniting with God's. When I say "heart" I am referring to that place in you where you are totally you. That place where your interior dialogue happens. That place that you reference when trying to describe how you feel to someone else, but can never seem to adequately describe it. Do you ever wonder why you cannot adequately describe it? It is because that place is not meant for any other creature in this world. It is made solely and completely for God. Our creator placed this in you as a cry for Him. It, from the beginning of you, has been crying out to Him.

On each of our hearts there is a throne. This throne we look to occupy with so many other things in our lives. But the only one who can occupy it, and actually bring peace to everything else, is our God and Savior Jesus Christ.

When Saint Paul exclaimed, "It is no longer I who live but Christ who lives in me," (Galatians 2:20) he was describing his heart completely and utterly occupied and ruled by Christ. This is the goal of our prayer lives and our spiritual journeys.

It is through prayer that Jesus starts to take His rightful place in our hearts, and eventually our lives.

*This place described in the first paragraph is what is commonly referred to as the interior life or the interior self. You will hear it commonly referred to as heart or soul as well throughout this resource.

PRAYER *(15 MINUTES MINIMUM)*

Note: These steps are meant to be gone through in a very slow, meditative, and prayerful way. Keep these things in your mind and repeat them until you feel them take hold in your heart.

Remember, these phrases and thoughts are just meant to help you if you don't know what to think or say. As you use these, you will begin to form phrases and thoughts that work better to condition your heart and mind to better enter into your relationship with God. After you go through them, move onto the Gospel reading and use the steps we learned on Day 5 as a guide.

> *"Come Holy Spirit."*

> *"God, I believe you are present here with me."*
> *(Rest on these words until you are aware of God's presence)*

> *"I believe this time that I have set aside to be with You means a lot to You, and that You will work in it."*

SETTING-UP THE PASSAGE: Jesus, after being tempted by Satan in the desert, and upon hearing of the arrest of John the Baptist, withdraws to the region of Galilee and begins his public ministry. He began in the synagogues, and his fame spread among the people there who were bringing their sick and dying to Him to be cured. Jesus then ascends to a hilltop and delivers the famous "Sermon on the Mount", which includes many teachings regarding the new covenant- more deeply revealing God's plan for humanity and how we are to be like Him. The following reading is among those teachings and it is in regards to prayer.

Matthew 6:5-8

[5]*"When you pray, do not be like the hypocrites, who love to stand and pray in the synagogues and on street corners so that others may see them. Amen, I say to you, they have received their reward. [6]But when you pray, go to your inner room, close the door, and pray to your Father in secret. And your Father who sees in secret will repay you. [7]In praying, do not babble like the pagans, who think that they will be heard because of their many words. [8]Do not be like them. Your Father knows what you need before you ask him.*

DAY 7: EXPLORING THE DEPTHS | THE INTERIOR LIFE

"Come Holy Spirit, inspire my heart and my mind. Bring me to the Heart of God."

CONSIDERATION

We have always known this interior place exists within us, but did we ever realize that it was made for someone specific? Did we ever consider that this place was actually loved by someone for our entire lives?

Today let's try to inspect our interior self. Let's contemplate what might be occupying that throne of our hearts. Maybe it already is Jesus, maybe it is not. In any case, if Jesus is already the ruler there, then chances are prayer is already a part of our lives. If we are claiming this but we are not taking the time to listen to Him, then it stands to reason we are not being truly honest with ourselves, and that He is taking a backseat to something else. You'd be surprised how much we can lie to ourselves within our thoughts; how we can actually trick ourselves to believe something that we know we made up. Well, this doesn't actually fool anyone – especially not ourselves. We know this because even when we answer that "Jesus" is the one who occupies that throne, we still don't feel peace there. If it truly is Jesus who occupies this throne, peace will reign strangely in the hardest of times, including those that otherwise would have caused great fear and anxiety.

So, as you go through this journey, realize that just as you can only fool yourself for so long with what happens interiorly, God has never been fooled. He sees through the interior tricks that you play. This is a good thing! We can be so caught up in creating the perfect alibi for ourselves that we miss sight of what would actually bring us healing – the truth. God is the truth. Allow His truth to penetrate this interior person – so broken and so wounded – and trust that, as a Father, this actually glorifies Him. Just like an earthly father, nothing brings God more joy than to see His children restored to Him.

PRAYER *(15 MINUTES MINIMUM)*

"Come Holy Spirit."

"God, I believe you are present here with me."
(Rest on these words until you are aware of God's presence)

"I believe this time that I have set aside to be with You means a lot to You, and that You will work in it."

SETTING-UP THE PASSAGE: Jesus has been questioned multiple times now by the Pharisees who are claiming that He is breaking old testament laws, and undermining God in doing so. Some of the more recent situations have involved Jesus' disciples picking grain to eat on the Sabbath as well as Jesus curing a man with a withered hand on the Sabbath.

Matthew 12: 22-30

23Then they brought to him a demoniac who was blind and mute. He cured the mute person so that he could speak and see. All the crowd was astounded, and said, "Could this perhaps be the Son of David?" 24But when the Pharisees heard this, they said, "This man drives out demons only by the power of Beelzebul, the prince of demons." 25But he knew what they were thinking and said to them, "Every kingdom divided against itself will be laid waste, and no town or house divided against itself will stand. 26And if Satan drives out Satan, he is divided against himself; how, then, will his kingdom stand? 27And if I drive out demons by Beelzebul, by whom do your own people* drive them out? Therefore they will *be your judges. [28]But if it is by the Spirit of God that I drive out demons, then the kingdom of God has come upon you. [29]How can anyone enter a strong man's house and steal his property, unless he first ties up the strong man? Then he can plunder his house. [30]Whoever is not with me is against me, and whoever does not gather with me scatters.*

DAY 8: IMAGE AND LIKENESS | THE INTERIOR LIFE

"Come Holy Spirit, inspire my heart and my mind. Bring me to the Heart of God."

CONSIDERATION

You have heard it said that we are made in the image and likeness of God (Genesis 1:27). Does this raise questions in you? How can we be made in the image of one who is pure spirit? Jesus now reigns with the Father in a glorified body, but there was a time before He was conceived in Mary's womb where He did not have a body; He existed then only as the Word of God. If you didn't have questions with the first statement, hopefully you do now.

The interior life that we have is the image and likeness of God that we were made in. Think about it: we can be separated within ourselves and even convince ourselves of something that is not so. It is like there are two dialogues happening within us. That being said, we can also be unified and feel fully ourselves. Now maybe you are saying, *"This is all well and good, but God is three in one, not two."* This is correct. The third person of God is the love the Father and Son share, known as the Holy Spirit. The Holy Spirit is the person of God who is to pull us into unity with Him so that, just as Jesus and the Father are one, we can be one as well. The Holy Spirit is the one who brings us the power of God to achieve oneness and peace.

It's interesting because you will find the more you present yourself to prayer, the more you see apparent hypocrisy in your old ways. You see yourself doing things that are self-contradicting, and you see ways in which those things can be amended. In other words, your heart starts melding with the heart of God and you become more unified like Him. Saint Paul says it well when he describes us as earthen vessels, in that when we are filled with God's love and truth in prayer, we will overflow, and virtue will be the mark of that overflowing (2 Corinthians 4:7).

However, when we do not seek God in prayer, we fill with things contrary to Him and our overflowing appears as vice.

It doesn't end here. This truth and our likeness to God goes much deeper. This understanding really helps our ability to realize He is our Father, and thus relate to Him all the more in prayer.

Ask Him to help you see Him better as your Father, and to see that you are truly His Son/Daughter. Ask Him to bring you to a better understanding of this, that it may well up within you and no longer be just a thought, but a conviction.

* If you look at the Genesis account of creation, you see that when God creates man the dialogue switches from singular "He" (meaning creation up to that point had been outside of Him) to a plural "Us": "Let us make man in Our own Image and Likeness…" (Gen. 1:26) Turning it into an interior dialogue within Himself points to the fact that we become like Him, multiple persons yet still one being, and that we hold a special place in the fact that He thought deeply of us, and in that thought we became like Him.

PRAYER *(15 MINUTES MINIMUM)*

> *"Come Holy Spirit."*

> *"God, I believe you are present here with me."*
> *(Rest on these words until you are aware of God's presence)*

> *"I believe this time that I have set aside to be with You means a lot to You, and that You will work in it."*

SETTING-UP THE PASSAGE: Jesus, after having celebrated the last supper with His disciples, begins telling them of the things to come: that He is about to leave, but His impending departure is necessary because the advocate (Holy Spirit) would be sent when He leaves. After instructing His disciples on these things, he raised the following prayer to His Father in heaven.

John 17:1-11

When Jesus had said this, he raised his eyes to heaven and said, "Father, the hour has come. Give glory to your son, so that your son may glorify you, [2] just as you gave him authority over all people, so that he may give eternal life to all you gave him. [3] Now this is eternal life, that they should know you, the only true God, and the one whom you sent, Jesus Christ. [4] I glorified you on earth by accomplishing the work that you gave me to do. [5] Now glorify me, Father, with you, with the glory that I had with you before the world began.

[6] "I revealed your name to those whom you gave me out of the world. They belonged to you, and you gave them to me, and they have kept your word. [7] Now they know that everything you gave me is from you, [8] because the words you gave to me I have given to them, and they accepted them and truly understood that I came from you, and they have believed that you sent me. [9] I pray for them. I do not pray for the world but for the ones you have given me, because they are yours, [10] and everything of mine is yours and everything of yours is mine, and I have been glorified in them. [11] And now I will no longer be in the world, but they are in the world, while I am coming to you. Holy Father, keep them in your name that you have given me, so that they may be one just as we are.

DAY 9: SIMPLY RELATIONAL | THE INTERIOR LIFE

"Come Holy Spirit, inspire my heart and my mind. Bring me to the Heart of God."

CONSIDERATION

One of the temptations we will face is to make our prayer with God something it is not. We will be tempted at times to make it more of an academic pursuit or a puzzle to be solved when, in fact, it is none of these things. Our God brings us what we desire most – simplicity. We tend to overcomplicate things when He just wants us to be with Him. We also tend to over emphasize things that may be good at the start, but our overemphasis makes them a distraction to what prayer really should be – a relationship.

This is the amazing thing about our God: He exists in a way in which He is not far from us if we approach Him in humility. Relating to Him is the most basic of things to grasp. But as it goes with us, we want to make it more about what we are doing and less about what He is doing. The fact is, everyone is capable of a relationship, and simplicity and good relationships go hand in hand.

A good example of the counter to this would be the state of the secular world today. The more we chase busyness the more we lose time for real intimate relationships; we say no to being with others because we are too busy with our worldly pursuits. We tend to keep them at a distance, which is one of the reasons we see things like social media become so popular; we like to push our busyness on our relationships, making them nothing more than a contact. We rarely have care-free time with each other; rather we prefer many of points of contact with those we care about, and we lie to ourselves and call that good enough.

Jesus sheds light on this in Matthew's Gospel when He says, "Father, I thank You, that You have hidden these things from the wise and understanding and revealed them to infants..." (Mattew 11:25).

How do infants have a relationship? It is completely in intimacy. There are no barriers thrown in the way of relating to an infant, no third parties, just being with them. Infants know how to receive and give intimacy. They enjoy simplicity.

Avoid the temptation to overcomplicate prayer. It is simply you coming to God relationally, trying to make yourself as open as possible to complete intimacy.

Spiritual maturity is allowing one's self to be an infant in the arms of the Father.

PRAYER *(15 MINUTES MINIMUM)*

> *"Come Holy Spirit."*
>
> *"God, I believe you are present here with me."*
> *(Rest on these words until you are aware of God's presence)*
>
> *"I believe this time that I have set aside to be with You means a lot to You, and that You will work in it."*

SETTING-UP THE PASSAGE: Jesus, after being questioned by the disciples of John the Baptist as to whether He was the messiah or not, replied to them referencing Old Testament prophesies of the messiah and showing how He had fulfilled them (blind receive sight, lame walk, etc...). He also spoke to the lack of repentance in the towns in which he had ministered. He then spoke the following to the crowds present.

Matthew 11:25-30

[25]*At that time Jesus said in reply, "I give praise to you, Father, Lord of heaven and earth, for although you have hidden these things from the wise and the learned you have revealed them to the childlike.* [26]*Yes, Father, such has been your gracious will.* [27]*All things have been handed over to me by my Father. No one knows the Son except the Father, and no one knows the Father except the Son and anyone to whom the Son wishes to reveal him.*

[28]*"Come to me, all you who labor and are burdened, and I will give you rest.* [29]*Take my yoke upon you and learn from me, for I am meek and humble of heart; and you will find rest for yourselves.* [30]*For my yoke is easy, and my burden light."*

DAY 10: OUR HEARTS RECOGNIZE HIM | THE INTERIOR LIFE

"Come Holy Spirit, inspire my heart and my mind. Bring me to the Heart of God."

CONSIDERATION

We often get caught up in the thought: "If only I could have been around when the first disciples were, then it would be so much easier to believe and have faith that God is there when I go to pray." Our eyes of faith really struggle at times.

It would be good to consider some accounts of encounters with Jesus shortly after His resurrection. These are, in many cases, deeply myste- rious. They seem odd, especially if the disciples of Jesus were trying to spread word of His rising and convince others to believe in the risen Jesus. Many of the accounts state that the disciples who encountered Him did not recognize Him at first. If we look specifically at the ac- count of the story of the Road the Emmaus, we see it was not until the breaking of the bread that the disciples recognized Jesus physically. Many find this to be a bit strange. Why does Jesus prefer to be so hid- den? I would argue here that Jesus does not prefer to remain hidden – in fact just the opposite. If you look further into these accounts, you will see that the disciples who were encountering Him recognized Him first in their hearts before He was physically revealed to them. This is specifically seen in the account of the Road to Emmaus when the disciples, recalling their walk with Jesus, exclaim to each other, "Were not our hearts burning within us while he spoke to us on the way and opened the scriptures to us?" (Luke 24:32) Is it possible we don't give God enough credit when we feel these stirrings in our heart?

This happens yet again in the account at the lake Genessarret as seven disciples were fishing. Jesus appeared to them, and as they were sitting down around a fire, Jesus said, "Come, have breakfast." None of the disciples dared to ask, "Who are you?" because they realized it was the Lord. (John 21:12) Why would they need to ask who He was if they recognized Him physically? Once again, in this example the disciples first recognized Him in their hearts. In fact, they didn't even question Him about His identity because His physical presence was not what revealed Him; it was His presence in their hearts that would keep them from asking if He was God. One could argue Jesus' presence with His disciples, after the resurrection, was even more intense than during his ministry before His crucifixion.

So what does all of this mean? This means that God is just as present to us today as He was with His disciples right after His resurrection. Today, like at that time, Jesus would rather reveal himself interiorly to us, and work within us. You see, our way of perceiving God is no different than it was for the disciples after His resurrection. When His physical presence was different, He continued to be revealed in the hearts of those who pursued Him and sought Him out. Jesus is as present to us today as He was after His resurrection with His disciples. The same Jesus is here, yet veiled to our eyes until He is enthroned in our hearts.

Today, imagine yourself on that road to Emmaus, and imagine what it must have felt like to have your heart burn with the Love only God can give. Let it awaken and foster a deep faith in the presence of God in your life today.

PRAYER *(15 MINUTES MINIMUM)*

> *"Come Holy Spirit."*

> *"God, I believe you are present here with me."*
> *(Rest on these words until you are aware of God's presence)*

> *"I believe this time that I have set aside to be with You means a lot to You, and that You will work in it."*

Luke 24:13-35

Now that very day two of them were going to a village seven miles from Jerusalem called Emmaus, [14]and they were conversing about all the things that had occurred. [15]And it happened that while they were conversing and debating, Jesus himself drew near and walked with them, [16]but their eyes were prevented from recognizing him. [17]He asked them, "What are you discussing as you walk along?" They stopped, looking downcast. [18]One of them, named Cleopas, said to him in reply, "Are you the only visitor to Jerusalem who does not know of the things that have taken place there in these days?" [19]And he replied to them, "What sort of things?" They said to him, "The things that happened to Jesus the Nazarene, who was a prophet mighty in deed and word before God and all the people, [20]how our chief priests and rulers both handed him over to a sentence of death and crucified him. [21]But we were hoping that he would be the one to redeem Israel; and besides all this, it is now the third day since this took place. [22]Some women from our group, however, have astounded us: they were at the tomb early in the morning [23]and did not find his body; they came back and reported that they had indeed seen a vision of angels who announced that he was alive. [24]Then some of those with us went to the tomb and found things just as the women had described, but him they did not see." [25]And he said to them, "Oh, how foolish you are! How slow of heart to believe all that the prophets spoke! [26]Was it not necessary that the Messiah should suffer these things and enter into his glory?" [27]Then beginning with Moses and all the prophets, he interpreted to them what referred to him in all the scriptures. [28]As they approached the village to which they were going, he gave the impression that he was going on farther. [29]But they urged him, "Stay with us, for it is nearly evening and the day is almost over." So he went in to stay with them. [30]And it happened that, while he was with them at table, he took bread, said the blessing, broke it, and gave it to them. [31]With that their eyes were opened and they recognized him, but he vanished from their sight. [32]Then they said to each other, "Were not our hearts burning [within us] while he spoke to us on the way and opened the scriptures to us?" [33]So they set out at once and returned to Jerusalem where they found gathered together the eleven and those with them [34]who were saying, "The Lord has truly been raised and has appeared to Simon!" [35]Then the two recounted what had taken place on the way and how he was made known to them in the breaking of the bread.

DAY 11: THE ATTRIBUTES OF GOD | THE INTERIOR LIFE

"Come Holy Spirit, inspire my heart and my mind. Bring me to the Heart of God."

CONSIDERATION

The interior life and its exploration in prayer lead us to encounter the attributes of God. It leads our hearts to a deep union with Him who created us. So deep is this union that He allows us into His heart to see its interior makings. If one could imagine the heart of God as the inner workings of an intricate hand clock, then prayer could be seen as our ability to go into that clock and look at all of the gears, seeing how one gear moves another, and how they work together in perfect balance with one not pushing the other beyond its means. This image points us to a deeper revelation about God and His attributes.

God is Love, which is the perfect balance of all virtue (divine and human) in an unmovable and unshakable being. Those gears we are exploring are divine virtue, and a Father's longing for His creation to come back to Him. You will see how Justice complements Mercy, and how all other virtues can work together if all held together by the glue which is Love itself – God the Father, Son, and Holy Spirit.

Contemplating the attributes of God allows us to see how we can amend our lives to be more like Him. It shows us how virtue needs to complement other virtue in our lives to achieve a life balance that is in honor of God, and not serving of ourselves. Like God, it is the thing that brings us to oneness of being. It is with this that hypocrisy, in the way we think or carry out our dealings, is uprooted; healthy roots form allowing us to image our creator in His non-contradicting and unified ways. In short, the more we present ourselves to Him, the more we become like Him, as He allows us into His interior being through meditation and contemplation.

PRAYER *(15 MINUTES MINIMUM)*

"Come Holy Spirit."

"God, I believe you are present here with me."
(Rest on these words until you are aware of God's presence)

"I believe this time that I have set aside to be with You means a lot to You, and that You will work in it."

SETTING-UP THE PASSAGE: Jesus, after being tempted by Satan in the desert, and upon hearing of the arrest of John the Baptist withdraws to the region of Galilee and begins his public ministry. He began in the synagogues, and his fame spread among the people who were bringing their sick and dying to Him to be cured. Jesus then ascends to a hilltop and delivers the following famously referred to as the "Sermon on the Mount" where he gives the beatitudes.

Matthew 5:3-12

When Jesus saw the crowds, he went up the mountain, and after he had sat down, his disciples came to him. He began to teach them, saying:
3"Blessed are the poor in spirit,
for theirs is the kingdom of heaven.
4Blessed are they who mourn,
for they will be comforted.
5Blessed are the meek,
for they will inherit the land.
6Blessed are they who hunger and thirst for righteousness,
for they will be satisfied.

[7]Blessed are the merciful,
for they will be shown mercy.
[8]Blessed are the clean of heart,
for they will see God.
[9]Blessed are the peacemakers,
for they will be called children of God.
[10]Blessed are they who are persecuted for the sake of righteousness,
for theirs is the kingdom of heaven.
[11]Blessed are you when they insult you and persecute you and utter every kind of evil against you [falsely] because of me.
[12]Rejoice and be glad, for your reward will be great in heaven. Thus they persecuted the prophets who were before you.

Note: The Ignatius Study Bible, *which is noted in the "Further Resources" Section, (pg. 59) has great footnotes that allow for better understanding of the beatitudes listed above.*

DAY 12: MARY: OUR MOTHER IN INTIMACY | THE INTERIOR LIFE

"Come Holy Spirit, inspire my heart and my mind. Bring me to the Heart of God."

CONSIDERATION

Our "yes" to God is very similar to Mary's "yes" to God when the Angel Gabriel appeared to her telling her that she would be the mother of the long awaited Messiah. Her "yes" brought the Word of God intimately within her, so much so that the word became flesh and started growing in her womb. Our "yes" to prayer does something similar. When the word of God comes into us through prayer, it dwells in us and grows within us to the point that it becomes as real in the spiritual sense as Jesus was in the physical sense in Mary's womb. We become spiritually impregnated – a new life forms within us. The very life of Jesus enters into us. Just as time split into two defined periods (B.C. and A.D.) when Jesus physically came into the world, you will be able to look back and see a split in your life as when you lived and when the word of God started living within you.

We hear in Luke's Gospel that after Mary had given birth to Jesus, and certain things were said to her regarding her son (like during His presentation into the temple) that, "Mary kept all these things, reflecting on them in Her heart" (Luke 2:8-20). In this way especially, she is our model of intimacy with God. We need to imitate her by reflecting on God's word, and the consolations He gives us in our hearts. Just as Mary contemplated her role in salvation quietly in her heart over time, so we must do the same.

Be confident that if you are coming to prayer, and are receiving the sacraments, that through the communion of Saints and the power of the Holy Spirit, you will be lead exactly where you need to be. Have confidence in what God gives you, testing it through discernment, but ultimately, like Mary, keeping it in your heart and reflecting on it. When it comes to be the right time, if you remain faithful like Mary, you will victoriously pass through the life circumstances that will be your cause for sainthood.

PRAYER *(15 MINUTES MINIMUM)*

"Come Holy Spirit."

"God, I believe you are present here with me."
(Rest on these words until you are aware of God's presence)

"I believe this time that I have set aside to be with You means a lot to You, and that You will work in it."

SETTING-UP THE PASSAGE: Mary and Joseph traveled to Bethlehem to be present for the census ordered by Caesar Augustus. When they arrived they found that there was no room for them in the lodges in the area so they stayed in a stable with the animals. There, Mary gave birth to Jesus.

Luke 2:8-20

Now there were shepherds in that region living in the fields and keeping the night watch over their flock. ⁹The angel of the Lord appeared to them and the glory of the Lord shone around them, and they were struck with great fear. ¹⁰The angel said to them, "Do not be afraid; for behold, I proclaim to you good news of great joy that will be for all the people. ¹¹For today in the city of David a savior has been born for you who is Messiah and Lord. ¹²And this will be a sign for you: you will find an infant wrapped in swaddling clothes and lying in a manger." ¹³And suddenly there was a multitude of the heavenly host with the angel, praising God and saying: [14]*"Glory to God in the highest and on earth peace to those on whom his favor rests."*

[15]*When the angels went away from them to heaven, the shepherds said to one another, "Let us go, then, to Bethlehem to see this thing that has taken place, which the Lord has made known to us."*

[16]*So they (shepherds) went in haste and found Mary and Joseph, and the infant lying in the manger.* [17]*When they saw this, they made known the message that had been told them about this child.* [18]*All who heard it were amazed by what had been told them by the shepherds.* [19]*And Mary kept all these things, reflecting on them in her heart.* [20]*Then the shepherds returned, glorifying and praising God for all they had heard and seen, just as it had been told to them.*

*If you have time through-out the day: Say a rosary going through the Joyful mysteries and, as you pray, ask Mary to help you understand the events you are meditating on. Ask that, like they did for her, they may take root in your heart.

DAY 13: THE WAY OF LIFE | THE INTERIOR LIFE

"Come Holy Spirit, inspire my heart and my mind. Bring me to the Heart of God."

CONSIDERATION

Because of my ultimate end, which is death, all of my dealings on earth, if they are completely my own, will be as cyanide tablets left for those who I am in contact with. My children (my own, or those who look to me as a role model) will taste sin through my teachings, and will ultimately receive the wage of sin: death. Left to my own devices I only have the power of death. Even what I claim to be "love" will ultimately be perverted to be serving of myself. My words will only quicken the decay of the one they are spoken to as their ultimate end too is death. This is because the mouth spews the overflow of the heart and mind.

The only way to truly live is to love through the One who conquered death – The Living One. In this way, our love and dealings with one another will ultimately bring life, because it is only in Jesus Christ that death was put to death. So although we ultimately die, our death, if in Christ, will be put to death and we will claim life in His name. It is not through our power that we can ever claim life as our end, but only in and through the most Holy name of Jesus Christ, and by entering into the mystery of His death and resurrection. May our lives ring of his passion so that, as we follow Him to death, we may also follow Him to eternal life.

It is only through a life of prayer (not forgoing the guide of the church and the sacraments), that we will come to know God intimately enough to claim this great gift of life that He has for us. Prayer is the way to start that interior revolution that fights sin and death within us, knocking them from the throne of our hearts, and replacing them with the Living One, Jesus Christ.

"It is no longer I who live but Christ who lives in me!" (Galatians 2:20)

Repeat this slowly and let it sink into your mind and heart:
"What hope do I have being one who is destined for death, but to cling to the Living One?"

PRAYER *(15 MINUTES MINIMUM)*

"Come Holy Spirit."

"God, I believe you are present here with me."
(Rest on these words until you are aware of God's presence)

"I believe this time that I have set aside to be with You means a lot to You, and that You will work in it."

SETTING-UP THE PASSAGE: Paul, is writing to the church in Corinth, which he helped to found through his missionary work, to spread the gospel to the Gentiles (those not of Jewish origin). He is addressing problems in the church there, and also teaching more in-depth the ways of God as revealed through Jesus Christ.

1 Corinthians 1:18-31

The message of the cross is foolishness to those who are perishing, but to us who are being saved it is the power of God. [19]*For it is written:*

"I will destroy the wisdom of the wise,
and the learning of the learned I will set aside."

[20]*Where is the wise one? Where is the scribe? Where is the debater of this age? Has not God made the wisdom of the world foolish?* [21]*For since in the wisdom of God the world did*

not come to know God through wisdom, it was the will of God through the foolishness of the proclamation to save those who have faith. ²²For Jews demand signs and Greeks look for wisdom, ²³but we proclaim Christ crucified, a stumbling block to Jews and foolishness to Gentiles, ²⁴but to those who are called, Jews and Greeks alike, Christ the power of God and the wisdom of God. ²⁵For the foolishness of God is wiser than human wisdom, and the weakness of God is stronger than human strength.

²⁶Consider your own calling, brothers. Not many of you were wise by human standards, not many were powerful, not many were of noble birth. ²⁷Rather, God chose the foolish of the world to shame the wise, and God chose the weak of the world to shame the strong, ²⁸and God chose the lowly and despised of the world, those who count for nothing, to reduce to nothing those who are something, ²⁹so that no human being might boast before God. ³⁰It is due to him that you are in Christ Jesus, who became for us wisdom from God, as well as righteousness, sanctification, and redemption, ³¹so that, as it is written, "Whoever boasts, should boast in the Lord."

DAY 14: PEACE | THE INTERIOR LIFE

"Come Holy Spirit, inspire my heart and my mind. Bring me to the Heart of God."

CONSIDERATION

The surest sign that God is working in you is an interior peace. Peace is the fruit and feeling of our Lord. This peace follows us through the most difficult times in our lives. If God is our anchor, peace is the rope that ties us to Him. Peace is our way of knowing the source of our meditation or contemplation. Peace is the reassurance that we are tied to our anchor: God.

Peace is different than typical emotions, because it does not leave in the midst of them. It is not something we can bring about; it is a grace God so lovingly gives to us. When natural fear grips us, peace can still be there. Fear and anxiety often occur as a result of not knowing what is awaiting us around the next bend of our lives. But peace can give the confidence to keep marching toward that bend with confidence in God and in His providence.

We will start to know peace more as we bear our hearts to God in prayer.

Today, ask Him for peace. Ask Him for a peace the world cannot give. Ask Him to start revealing that peace to you, especially during your time of prayer, so that you may know its source as it follows you throughout the day.

PRAYER *(15 MINUTES MINIMUM)*

> *"Come Holy Spirit."*
>
> *"God, I believe you are present here with me."*
> *(Rest on these words until you are aware of God's presence)*
>
> *"I believe this time that I have set aside to be with You means a lot to You, and that You will work in it."*

SETTING-UP THE PASSAGE: Jesus, after having celebrated the last supper with His disciples, begins telling them of the things to come, that He is about to leave, but His impending departure is necessary because the advocate (Holy Spirit) would be sent when He leaves.

John 14:23-29

Jesus answered and said to him, "Whoever loves me will keep my word, and my Father will love him, and we will come to him and make our dwelling with him. 24Whoever does not love me does not keep my words; yet the word you hear is not mine but that of the Father who sent me.

[25]*"I have told you this while I am with you.* [26]*The Advocate, the Holy Spirit that the Father will send in my name—he will teach you everything and remind you of all that [I] told you.* [27]*Peace I leave with you; my peace I give to you. Not as the world gives do I give it to you. Do not let your hearts be troubled or afraid.* [28]*You heard me tell you, 'I am going away and I will come back to you.' If you loved me, you would rejoice that I am going to the Father; for the Father is greater than I.* [29]*And now I have told you this before it happens, so that when it happens you may believe.*

REVOLUTION does not happen on a battlefield or in a courtroom or outside of one's self. It happens in the very constructs of the human heart and mind that is given over to prayer and contemplation of the one that created them.

Prayer ignites a revolution.

A WAY FORWARD

Enthroned is not something to be done and then cast aside; rather, it is meant to be the jumpstart to a new way of life. It is important that you stay the course of prayer and continue to let God mold you and shape you from the inside. Continue to let Him speak to your heart by giving Him your undivided attention during some part of the day, and you will see that your life will be forever changed for the better.

A good way forward from here is to practice Lectio Divina (the steps from day 5) on the daily readings that the church lays out in the liturgical calendar. There is a reading and gospel for every day, and in the course of about 3 years you will cover almost the entire Bible. That means that if you stay the course, you will have prayed through most of God's word! What an amazing thing. This word will transform you, and God will speak to you when you meditate and pray on it.

Please do not lose hope in this journey. Through prayer, your love will be empowered to be more like the Father's love, and through this process you will become a saint and will transform the world for the better. Just focus on taking it day by day; when you fall get back up, and find others who will help you along the journey.

Be assured of my prayers for you and your prayer life, that it may flourish and that God may take the throne of your heart.

THE IMPORTANCE OF STUDY

In my experience in helping others in their prayer life and spiritual journey, I have found a common item that leads to lack of belief and dryness in prayer: a lack of continued study of the faith. I know from my own experience that when my study and reading wanes, so does my fervor to come to prayer and to grow toward God. If we take a look at the realities of our state on this earth, it is not hard to see why this is the case.

The devil loves to put things in our head that make us think that God is in competition with us. He loves to bind us to our sin and tell us that God couldn't possibly love us for who we are because of it. While it is true, that sin distances our relationship with God, the distancing only exists on our end, not on God's. Think of the parable of the good shepherd who, when the sheep wanders off (notice it is not the shepherd who wanders) the shepherd goes in search of Him and carries the sheep back on His shoulders. If we stray from reading and studying more about God revealed through Jesus, the saints, and the church, then we stand to fall prey to the lies and untruths of the evil one. The reading and studying of our faith, and the person of God, deepen the truths which we can bring to prayer. God builds on these truths and beautifies them in Himself when they are meditated on and brought to Him.

Study does not have to be hard. Just something as simple as reading 15 minutes a day from a Christian book can do so much. If you need help finding good resources, there are some at the end of this book, but you can always go to your priest and ask for recommendations.

So when you are experiencing dryness or discouragement, think of looking for inspiration in the many resources of the Church and Saints to increase your vision of God, and thus deepen your prayer and relationship with Him.

THE IMPORTANCE OF GOOD COUNSEL

Prayer creates conviction in us. This conviction is what drives us to do the things in our life more boldly for Jesus and the spread of the Gospel. This boldness is great and is absolutely essential if we are to become who we are meant to be. Just like anything though, this also needs to be in check. This boldness can swell in us and actually serve to move us toward pride, and the more that happens the more the devil can get in, causing our boldness to bend toward serving his will. Our pride fogs our vision of God, and this pride seems to come in and out like the tide. It sneaks in slowly, almost unnoticed, until we find ourselves doing something that seems more blatantly against what we thought we stood for. This normally shows its face in the surfacing of more serious sin.

After reading this you may be tempted to say, "if prayer is so danger-ous, and may actually embolden me for the enemy, why even take the chance?" Good question. There are several remedies, but I have found the most effective to be seeking good counsel from people whose fruits (actions, dealings) would suggest they are on the right path.

Personally, I have a men's group that meets once a month. I also have a personal accountability meeting with a friend who is committed to prayer and the message of the gospel. This meeting happens once a week before we both go to work, so it is not taxing on my family life. I cannot begin to tell you how many times this meeting has helped me work through things that were starting to become tainted with my pride, and areas where I was starting to let the devil in.

This is absolutely essential. If you are not able to do all of these things, do not omit prayer, but rather seek out good counsel when you can, and try to consider where others may be coming from when they seem opposed to your view on things. If we write others off, then we are possibly writing off the council that God is sending us to get back on His path. It is all in the fruits. Listen to those who sow peace and love in the world. They are your allies.

Proverbs 12:15

"The way of fools is right in their own eyes, but those who listen to advice are the wise."

AN EXHORTATION OF A WEARY HEART

OH, LITTLE WEAK HEART

Praise be to God! My love for you overflows
You pour yourself into me but I do not have
enough room, so You overflow.
You pour more it seems than my current lot would suggest
You are gracious and generous
Your love carries me through the day and stirs my heart to
love of You during the night
So much more than I am are You
You stir and I dance
So much for such a little weak heart, so much

*But little weak heart, when the dance slows
and the waters do not run over,
do you forget?
Are you but an instance only to remember the current time?
Is it possible that your King has moved on?
His promises, are they now not to be believed?*

Little weak heart, forge ahead
Believe what was spoken to you, do not lose your grip on reality
Your God does not falter, nor can He act outside of His word
My dear weak heart, you cannot limit God to your state,
you must allow Him to be
His ways are so high above your own
He draws you through the valleys so that you may not falter at the peaks
He draws back so you realize your limits; to not suffer the fault of
self-reliance in the face of too great a task

He draws back to work deeper
Oh little weak heart, you know He loves you so
With the stirrings, little though they may be, choose to dance
Choose to love when you are not overflowing and
your God will be well pleased
He invites you to pursue a heart pierced but acting
still in love, like His own
You are to be like Him
Oh little weak heart, learn well
Do not relinquish your trust, but give it to Him all the more
For trust in Him transforms you from within

FURTHER RESOURCES

Once God starts to take the throne of a heart, that heart turns to the narrow road of the cross and seeks to walk it. This reference area is here to let you know of other resources that can tell you of the constants on that road so that, when your prayer is hard, you do not give up: instead, rely on the constants and what you know to be true. It is important that we know this path is well trod, and that those that have gone before us have left us many valuable helps and resources to effectively navigate this road.

There is a point for every traveler where he must go back to the basics to make the next turn.

Ignatius Catholic Study Bible: New Testament
Ignatius Press (Curtis Mitch and Scott Hahn)
Description: This bible is truly a gift to our modern age as we have lost so much of the context of the life and times of Jesus and the traditions of the Jewish people which are the roots of our faith. This bible has footnotes and studies in it that provide contextual understanding and church-guided interpretation of the readings. It is an indispensable tool for learning the New Testament scriptures.

The Catechism of the Catholic Church
Section on Prayer starts: CCC 2558 (Section Four)
Description: This is one of the best all-around resources for prayer, from exploration of the interior life, to mechanics, to scriptural references, and increased understanding it is an excellent and beautifully written resource and it has the added benefit of the authority of the Church.

An Introduction to the Devout Life
St Francis DeSales
Description: This is a very powerful work for the laity. It is a help to prayer, devotion, and then Christian walk in general. It is focused mostly on the lifelong disciplines that will help a Christian achieve a devotion worthy of sanctity. This book changed my life.

The Three Conversions in the Spiritual Life
Fr. Reginald Garrigou-Lagrange, O.P.
Description: I cannot overstate the importance of reading about the stages of the spiritual life. So often the reason people stop praying is because of time of darkness where it seems as though God has left. Learning about the spiritual life will help you to see that the dryer/darker times are just as important as the times of consolation and communion, and as such will empower you to continue on your journey in prayer toward God.

WORKS CITED

Catholic Church. (1997). *Catechism of the Catholic Church: Revised in accordance with the official Latin text promulgated by Pope John Paul II* (2nd ed.). Washington, D.C.: United States Catholic Conference.

New American Bible, revised edition© 2010, 1991, 1986, 1970 Confraternity of Christian Doctrine, Washington, D.C.

Pope Benedict XVI. *Jesus of Nazareth: The Infancy Narratives.* Translated by Philip J. Whitmore, Image, 2012.

"Relativism." *Merriam-Webster,* 20 Jan. 2017
www.merriam-webster.com/dictionary/relativism

"The Ladder of Four Rungs – Guigo II on Contemplation." *Ultima,* 21 April. 2017
http://www.umilta.net/ladder.html